Thank You for the MUSIC

A Celebration OF THE VALUE OF Creativity

ADMIT ONE

ARENA TICKET
ROW 38 SEAT 149

A Practical Guide to Music

NoodleJUiCE

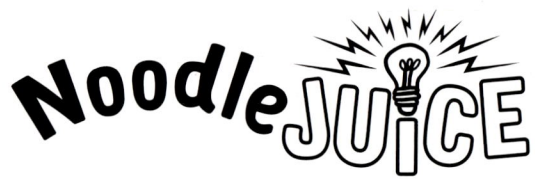

Noodle Juice Ltd

www.noodle-juice.com

Stonesfield House, Stanwell Lane, Great Bourton, Oxfordshire, OX17 1QS

First published in Great Britain 2024

Copyright © Noodle Juice Ltd 2024

Text by Sarah Walden 2022

Illustrations by Hannah Li 2023

All rights reserved

Printed in China

A CIP catalogue record of this book is available from the British Library

ISBN: 978-1-915613-18-9

1 3 5 7 9 10 8 6 4 2

FSC
www.fsc.org
MIX
Paper | Supporting
responsible forestry
FSC® C005748

This book is made from
FSC®-certified paper.
By choosing this book,
you help to take care of
the world's forests.
Learn more: www.fsc.org.

So I say
Thank you for the music, the songs I'm singing
Thanks for all the joy they're bringing.
Who can live without it? I ask in all honesty
What would life be?
Without a song or a dance, what are we?
So I say thank you for the music
For giving it to me.

Benny Goran Bror Andersson / Bjoern K. Ulvaeus, *ABBA*

'Thank You for the Music' lyrics © EMI Music Publishing, France

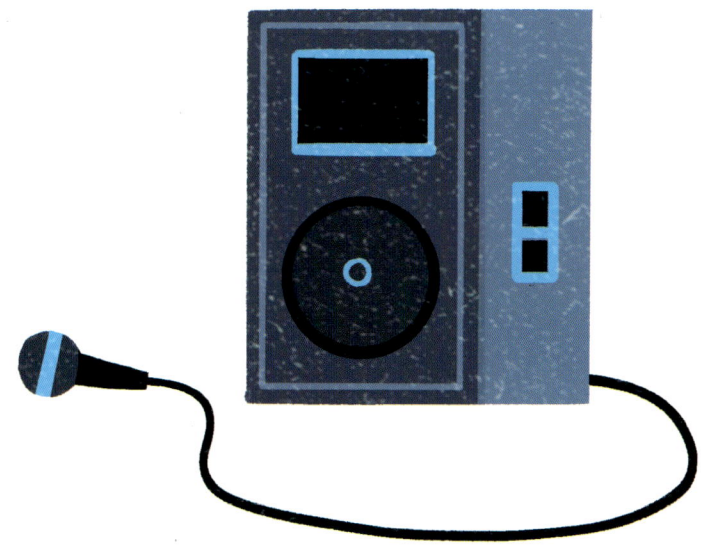

Music ... can name the unnameable, and communicate the unknowable.

Leonard Bernstein, composer

Contents

6   What is music?

8   Classical music
10 Orchestral voices
12 Meet the string family
14 Blow, wind, blow…
16 Crash, bang, wallop!
18 Famous classical composers

20 20th century music
22 Let's rock!
24 Pop central
26 It's a little bit country
28 Rhythm is here to stay
30 Music from around the world

34 The sound of music
36 What an atmosphere!
38 And try that one more time…

40 Careers in music
42 Musical artist
44 Composer

45 Songwriter
46 DJ
47 Radio producer
48 Musical director
50 Music agent
52 Music producer
54 Concert promoter
55 Tour manager
56 Sound engineer
58 Music tutor
60 Music therapist
62 Music journalist

64 How to create music
66 How to write a song
68 How to record a piece of music
70 How to form a band
72 How to put on a music gig
74 How to get started…

76 Further reading
78 Index

What is music?

Music is when sounds, either vocal, rhythmic or instrumental, or all three, are arranged in a combination that sounds pleasing to the ear. Often music expresses emotion.

Music exists in every human society in one form or another. You can combine music with words to create songs, or with movement to create dance. Music can also impact how you feel.

Music is created from three key elements.

tzz, tzz, tzz

rat-a-tat-tat

bang, bang, bang

Rhythm

Repeated patterns normally played by percussion, such as drums, or bass instruments.

Melody

Single notes which follow each other to create a tune that is enjoyable to hear.

Harmony

Multiple notes played or sung at the same time which combine to create a pleasing sound.

Music can sometimes be extravagant and celebrational using a full symphony orchestra and choir.

It can also be a singer with a guitar busking on the street.

There are lots of different kinds of music and different countries have their own musical traditions. The music industry is a fascinating world that requires a huge number of people in many different roles to make music that we can listen to on our phones, computers and record players or in fields, halls and arenas.

Turn the page to discover more!

Classical music

During the medievel period, most formally composed music was used in a religious setting. Secular — non-religious music or the medievel version of pop music — was mainly limited to troubadours who roamed the land singing songs of love and war, as well as sharing topical events.

It wasn't until the 17th century that the style of classical music you can hear today began to appear.

Musical instruments were more sophisticated and allowed for more complex compositions. Composers started to produce works such as 'sonatas' or 'concertos' which allowed different instrumental groups to provide a variety of musical textures in quartets or orchestras.

Orchestral voices

A symphony orchestra has many different musicians playing lots of different instruments to create the complex and layered music created by composers such as Beethoven, Rachmaninoff or Gershwin.

This is a typical plan showing where each musican would sit.

Percussion

Horns

Harp

Clarinets

2nd Violins

Piccolo & flutes

1st Violins

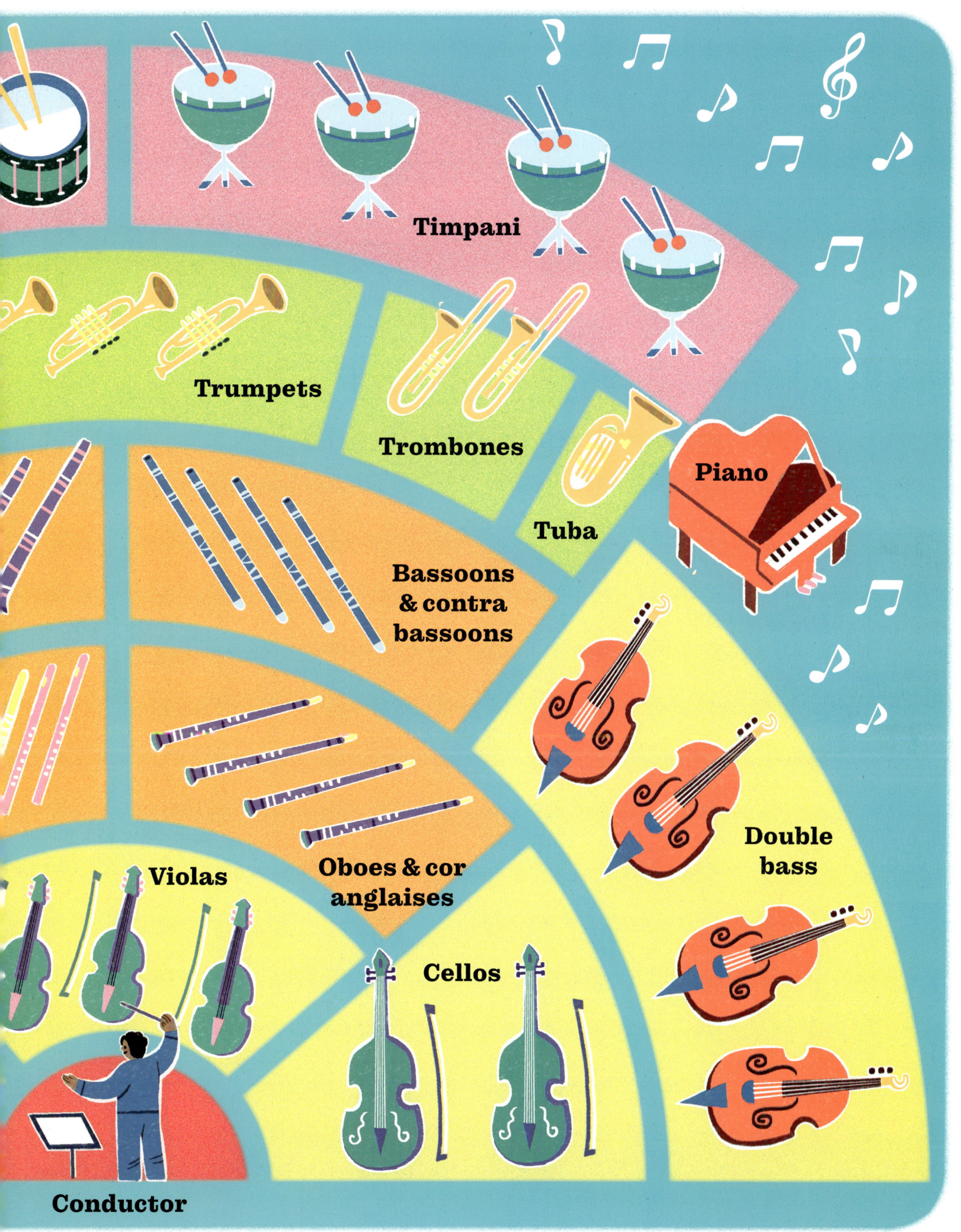

Timpani

Trumpets

Trombones

Tuba

Piano

Bassoons & contra bassoons

Double bass

Violas

Oboes & cor anglaises

Cellos

Conductor

Meet the string family

Stringed instruments are any instrument that makes a sound from the vibrations of a stretched string made from gut, metal or nylon. The sound of the string is made louder by an amplifying board and the string can be plucked, bowed or struck to make it vibrate and produce a sound.

Early string instruments

These include lutes, zithers, lyres and harps, and are often pictured in medieval or Chinese art. The only continent that doesn't appear to have used string instruments is the Americas before the Europeans arrived.

Piano

Technically a piano is a stringed instrument, although you might not think so to look at them. But hidden in the wooden frame are many strings that are struck by hammers whenever a piano key is pressed down.

The violin family

There are four members of the violin family which give a full and dramatic sound in a symphony orchestra. These range in size from the large double bass which often provides the undertones and foundation of rhythm, especially in jazz music, to the violin with a much higher range of notes. Their strings can be plucked, or played with a bow to create a lush, romantic sound.

Violin

Also known as a fiddle, the violin is one of the most popular instruments to play. Tucked under the chin, one hand supports the violin so that the fingers on that hand can be used to change notes on the strings. The other hand is then used to draw the bow across the strings to make a sound.

Cello

The cello provides a rich bass sound. Held between the cellist's legs, the player's left hand presses on the strings to create notes, and the right hand can use the bow or pluck the strings.

Viola

A viola is slightly bigger than the violin, so it produces a richer, lower range of notes.

Double bass

The largest member of the violin family. this instrument plays notes a whole octave below those of the cello. The double bass is not just used for classical music, and can be found in the rhythm section of most jazz bands.

Blow, wind, blow...

There are two different types of wind instruments in classical music. The woodwind section which includes flutes, clarinets, oboes, bassoons and saxophones, and the brass wind section made up of trumpets, trombones, horns and the tuba.

Flute and piccolo

The flute, and its smaller relative the piccolo, have existed in some form since the second century BCE. Held horizontally to the right of the player, the musician blows across the flute's mouthpiece to create its distinctive 'wobbly' sound.

Oboe

The oboe has a double reed mouthpiece which the player blows through. Invented in the mid 17th century, it is the main woodwind instrument in a symphony orchestra and has many solo parts written for it.

Clarinet and saxophone

The clarinet and saxophone both use a single reed mouthpiece. While both instruments are part of a symphony orchestra, the saxphone is more prominent in jazz music.

Bassoon

Providing the bass element of the woodwind family, the bassoon also has a double reed. This is one of the harder woodwind instruments to master due to the complex placement of the fingerholes.

Trumpet

Played using the lips to vibrate against the mouthpiece, the trumpet dates from the second millennium BCE in Egypt. The modern valve trumpet was invented in the early 19th century.

Trombone

Played similarly to the trumpet, the trombone has a slide rather than valves. This means the player can 'swoop' from one note to the next, creating a distinctive sound. It used to be known as the 'sackbut'.

Horn

The horn, originally used for hunting, has a coiled body with a large bell. The player can change the sound of the notes by inserting their hand or a cone into the bell.

Tuba

The tuba is the largest brass instrument and is capable of producing very low notes indeed. Often used in military bands, the tuba is carried in front of the body with its wide bell carried above the player's head.

Crash, bang, wallop!

Percussion instruments are split into two types. One type, such as a drum, has a membrane that is stretched over a frame which is then hit. The other type, such as a bell or rattle, is moved by the player to create a sound. Typically, the percussion family provides the rhythm in classical music, and is often known as the 'rhythm section'.

Another way to group percussion instruments is by whether they are tuned, such as a glockenspiel, or not, such as a snare drum. Both are hit by beaters or sticks.

Castanets, clappers and cymbals

These members of the percussion family consist of two parts which are struck together to create sound. In classical music, a pair of castanets is held in each hand. Cymbals can range in size and produce a very impressive noise. They are often used in marching bands.

Xylophones

Consisting of different size wooden bars, arranged in pitch order from left to right, a xylophone is played using sticks or mallets. A similar instrument made of metal bars is called the glockenspiel.

Tubular chimes

Tubular chimes or bells are the most musical of the percussion instruments. The hanging metal tubes are struck with a hammer to create a sound similar to church bells.

Rattles

As the name suggests, these instruments create rhythmic sounds when shaken. Various vessels made from different materials mean there is a wide choice of sound to choose from.

Triangles

Often the first instrument anyone plays, the triangle and other simliar instruments are struck to create a single note.

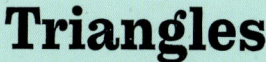

Drums

There are three main types of drum. Kettle drums or 'timpani' can be tuned by tightening the membrane. Friction drums such as a 'snare drum' use friction to create their sound. Finally, there are pot drums, which can be found in Africa, Asia and the Americas.

Famous classical composers

Here is a timeline of some of the most significant Western composers. How many have you heard of?

Georges Bizet
1838-1875
French

Camille Saint-Saëns
1835-1921
French

Antonio Vivaldi
1678-1741
Italian

Franz Joseph Haydn
1732-1809
Austrian

Johannes Brahms
1833-1897
German

Johann Sebastian Bach
1685-1750
German

Wolfgang Amadeus Mozart
1756-1791
Austrian

Clara Schumann
1819-1896
German

George Frideric Handel
1685-1759
German-British

Ludwig van Beethoven
1770-1827
German

Richard Wagner
1813-1883
German

Johann Pachelbel
1653-1706
German

Gioachino Rossini
1792-1868
Italian

Guiseppe Verdi
1813-1901
Italian

Barbara Strozzi
1619-1677
Italian

Franz Schubert
1797-1828
Austrian

Thomas Tallis
1505-1585
British

Fanny Mendelssohn
1805-1847
German

Frédéric Chopin
1810-1849
Polish

Hildegard of Bingen
1098-1179
German

Felix Mendelssohn
1809-1847
German

Robert Schumann
1810-1856
German

Modest Mussorgsky
1839–1881
Russian

Benjamin Britten
1913–1976
British

Dimitri Shostakovitch
1906–1975
Russian

Peter Ilyich Tchaikovsky
1840–1893
Russian

Leonard Bernstein
1918–1990
American

Aaron Copland
1900–1990
American

Antonín Dvořák
1841–1904
Austrian

John Williams
1932–
American

Eduard Grieg
1843–1907
Norwegian

Lili Boulanger
1893–1918
French

Philip Glass
1937–
American

Edward Elgar
1857–1934
British

Sergei Prokofiev
1891–1953
Russian

Hans Zimmer
1957–
German

Ethel Smyth
1858–1944
British

Florence Price
1887–1953
American

Kerry Andrew
1978–
British

Giacomo Puccini
1858–1924
Italian

Igor Stravinksy
1882–1971
Russian

Claude Débussy
1862–1918
French

Maurice Ravel
1875–1937
French

Richard Strauss
1864–1949
German

Gustav Holst
1874–1934
British

Jean Sibelius
1865–1957
Finnish

Sergei Rachmaninoff
1873–1943
Russian

Amy Beach
1867–1944
American

Ralph Vaughan Williams
1872–1958
British

20th century music

A more informal type of music grew out of the troubadour movement. Known as folk music, because it kept traditional oral songs alive, this was the music listened to by working people.

By the late 19th century, popular music had taken the place of folk music.

Pop music was very much of its time and place and was supported by the invention of the record player. Ragtime, jazz and country music were played on radios across America. Rock 'n' roll, Motown, soul, reggae and disco followed, leading to today's musical movements of pop, funk, hip hop and rap.

With the advent of streaming, it is possible for someone to listen to any genre of music. 21st century music fans can hear songs from the 1930s, 1970s or 2010s at the press of a button.

Let's rock!

Rock 'n' roll music first appeared in the 1950s. Using guitars, drums and charismatic lead singers, often with a backing group, this exciting new musical style took off with a young man from Memphis, USA, called Elvis Presley.

Elvis Presley's most famous songs

A Little Less Conversation
All Shook Up
Always on My Mind
Are You Lonesome Tonight?
Blue Christmas
Blue Suede Shoes
Can't Help Falling in Love
Heartbreak Hotel
In the Ghetto
Jailhouse Rock
Love Me Tender
Return to Sender
Hound Dog
Suspicious Minds
The Wonder of You
Viva Las Vegas

It wasn't just Elvis Presley making the charts though with rock 'n' roll. Performers such as Fats Domino, Buddy Holly, Little Richard, Chuck Berry, Eddie Cochran and Jerry Lee Lewis all benefitted from a new audience – the American teenager.

By the 1960s, however, the rock 'n' roll sound had moved on with more sophisticated techniques and recording styles.

Enter the world of rock!

The Beatles from Liverpool, UK, were the next global rock phenomenon. John, Paul, George and Ringo were the most important muscians of the 1960s, eclipsing all other music artists in terms of screaming fans.

The Beatles most famous songs

A Hard Day's Night
All You Need Is Love
Can't Buy Me Love
Eleanor Rigby
Hey Jude
Help!
I Want to Hold Your Hand
Let It Be
We Can Work It Out
Yellow Submarine
Yesterday

The Rolling Stones swiftly followed the Beatles across the Atlantic and enjoyed huge success with songs such as '(I Can't Get No) Satisfaction' and 'Get Off of My Cloud.'

Jimi Hendrix was a talented electric guitarist and used his skills with an amplifier to create a new sound. He can be credited with giving fans their first stadium concerts and outdoor festivals.

By the 1980s, rock had diversified into different strands, often based around a specific city or youth culture.

Grunge (Seattle, US)

Alice In Chains, Mudhoney, Nirvana, Pearl Jam, Soundgarden, Stone Temple Pilots

Heavy metal (global)

AC/DC, Anthrax, Black Sabbath, Iron Maiden, Led Zeppelin, Motorhead, Metallica, Motley Crue

Punk (UK/US)

Blink-182, The Clash, The Damned, Green Day, The Ramones, Sex Pistols

Britpop (UK)

Blur, Oasis, Pulp, Supergrass

Progressive Rock (UK)

Emerson, Lake and Palmer, Genesis, Pink Floyd, Rush, Yes

Popular rock bands today sell out stadium tours around the world.

Arctic Monkeys, Beck, Coldplay, Evanescence, Foo Fighters, Green Day, Linkin Park, The Killers, Kings of Leon, Muse, OneRepublic, Paramore, Radiohead, Red Hot Chilli Peppers, Train, The Strokes, U2

Pop central

Pop music, originally used to describe all forms of 'popular' music, has come to represent what is seen as commercial and accessible music in the USA and Great Britain. It appeals to a very broad audience, although it is often considered to be more popular with younger people.

What makes a pop song?

Pop music is characterised by having an upbeat, danceable rhythm. Pop songs also often have easy to remember lyrics, and can be called 'anthems'. The structure of a pop song is also simple, with verses and a repeated, recognisable chorus.

Famous pop singers

There are many globally famous British and American pop stars. Here are a few from the last 50 years. How many have you heard of?

Justin Timberlake

Jennifer Lopez

Whitney Houston

Prince

Britney Spears

Taylor Swift

Cher

Adele

Ed Sheeran

Madonna

Elton John

Lady Gaga

Justin Bieber

Beyoncé

Disco

Hugely popular dance music from the 1970s, disco takes its name from the word *discotheque*, the word for dance clubs that started appearing in the late 1960s. DJs playing sets in these nightclubs helped to make this kind of music popular.

Well-known disco tracks

Don't Leave Me This Way – Thelma Houston, 1976

Hot Stuff – Donna Summer, 1979

In the Navy – Village People, 1979

I Will Survive – Gloria Gaynor, 1978

Le Freak – Chic, 1978

Stayin' Alive – The Bee Gees, 1977

Never Can Say Goodbye – Gloria Gaynor, 1974

We Are Family – Sister Sledge, 1979

K-Pop

Korean popular music took the world by storm in the 21st century. PSY's 'Gangnam Style' topped the charts globally, but the most popular Korean artists are boy bands such as BTS and Enhypen. Their stunning dance choreography and slick outfits proved popular all over the world. K-Pop bands sometimes can have up to as many as 17 members at a time.

It's a little bit country

Country music

This type of music comes from Southern and Midwestern America. Made popular by local radio stations during the 1930s, songs featured the fiddle, guitar and banjo. Country musicians sang about poverty and loneliness, appealing to their largely poor audience. Its popularity spread across the whole of the USA after World War II, and Nashville, Tennessee, became the centre for country music recording and performance. Now a huge commercial operation, performers such as Dolly Parton, Garth Brooks and Carrie Underwood regularly top the US Billboard charts.

Best-selling country musicians

Alabama

Alan Jackson

Dolly Parton

Garth Brooks

George Strait

Kenny Rogers

Reba McEntire

Shania Twain

Taylor Swift

Folk music

One of the oldest forms of popular music, folk tunes have been revived and collected by many musicians. Some, such as Pete Seeger in the late 20th century, used their music to send a message, protesting against war or racial discrimination. Folk music today is characterised by the use of acoustic (non-electronic) instruments and vocal harmonies.

Jazz

Developed in the late 19ᵗʰ and early 20ᵗʰ century in New Orleans, USA, by African Americans, jazz music combines African rhythms and European harmonies. Often improvised (meaning composed at the time of playing), jazz also calls on blues music and ragtime dance themes. Key instruments for jazz players include the trumpet, the trombone, the saxophone, the double bass and the piano.

Famous jazz soloists

Bessie Smith

Billie Holliday

Charlie Parker

Duke Ellington

John Coltrane

Louis Armstrong

Miles Davis

Nat King Cole

Soul music

Used to describe African American popular music between the 1960s and 1970s. Soul music draws from gospel music and blues, as well as funk rhythms. A key characteristic is a powerful vocal lead, as well as the use of call and response. Well-known soul singers include Aretha Franklin, Wilson Pickett, Otis Redding and James Brown.

Motown music is also considered to be soul music. Artists such as Marvin Gaye, Stevie Wonder and the Supremes grew in popularity as the Motown record label tried to appeal to white teenagers.

Both soul and Motown songs were often used to convey a political message.

Records with a message

Can I Get A Witness?
Marvin Gaye, 1963

A Change Is Gonna Come
Sam Cooke, 1964

Say It Loud – I'm Black and I'm Proud (Part 1)
James Brown, 1968

Everyday People
Sly and the Family Stone, 1968

War
Edwin Starr, 1970

Rhythm is here to stay

Rap music

This music genre owes more to rhythm than melody. The lyrics are chanted or rapped to backing music, often created by sampling other musical recordings. Originating from African American communities in New York in the late 1970s and early 1980s, rap music can be divisive as its lyrics are often considered to glamorise drugs and violence.

Old school

DJ Kool Herc

Grandmaster Flash

Sugar Hill Gang

New school

50 Cent

Beastie Boys

Diddy

Eminem

Fugees

Ice Cube

Jay-Z

Kanye West

Lauryn Hill

LL Cool J

M.I.A.

Public Enemy

Queen Latifah

Run-D.M.C

Salt-N-Pepa

Snoop Dogg

Hip hop

Closely associated with rap music, hip hop is a cultural style that includes DJing, rapping, graffiti and dance. DJs use two turntables to mix tunes and percussive elements together to create a constant stream of music for their dancing audience. Drawing on funk rhythms, new school hip hop became the background beat for most American dance music of the 1990s.

Ska

An extremely rhythmic style of music, ska developed in Jamaica in the 1950s. By mixing Caribbean folk music such as the Cuban mambo and the Jamaican mento with the boogie-woogie New Orleans piano style, ska developed as a new 'off-beat' rhythm. Ska was particularly popular in Britain and bands such as Madness, the Clash and the Specials used its high-energy four-beat rhythms to huge success.

Ska hits

My Boy Lollipop
Millie Small, 1964

007 (Shanty Town)
Desmond Dekker &
The Aces, 1968

One Step Beyond
Madness, 1979

Ghost Town
The Specials, 1979

London Calling
The Clash, 1979

Reggae music

Originating in Jamaica in the 1960s as an offshoot to ska, reggae music quickly spread internationally and by the 1970s it was popular in the United States, Britain and Africa. Taking the same four-beat pattern with drums and bass guitar, but using a guitar to represent the sounds of gunshots in the streets, reggae music was meant to express the sounds of Jamaican gangster culture. It also conveyed a political message highlighting social and economic inequality. Well-known reggae artists include Bob Marley and the Wailers, Jimmy Cliff, Desmon Dekker, Toots and the Maytals, Steel Pulse and UB40.

Bob Marley's greatest hits

Buffalo Soldier

Get Up, Stand Up

I Shot the Sheriff

No Woman No Cry

One Love

Redemption Song

Three Little Birds

Music from around the world

The major musical genres we've discussed already have an international reach, but every country in the world has its own musical tradition. Here are some more musical styles and instruments to consider.

Chinese music can be traced back to 3000 BCE. Their famous operas date from the 12th century and the most popular form is *jingxi*, known as Peking opera.

There are many, many different types of African music, but common instruments to most are drums and flutes. Different African tribes use different stringed instruments such as zithers, harps, lutes and lyres.

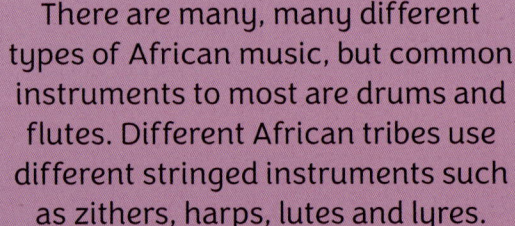

Traditional Korean music uses a drum, called a *changgo*, which is hour-glass shaped. The musician uses their left hand to beat the drum on one side and a stick in their right hand to hit the other.

Traditional Spanish music is played for their famous flamenco dancers. Instruments such as tambourines and wooden castanets accompany the singer as they sing.

Polynesian music is also closely linked to dancing. Often, the performer will depict a mythical being, such as a god or monster, by wearing an elaborate mask and costume.

Indian music is divided into *ragas* or different types of melody. The instruments used to play a raga consist of drums such as the *tabla*, and stringed instruments such as the *sitar* and the *tambura*.

Islamic music is usually performed by a single musician. The singer often improvises substantially within the piece of music they are singing.

The *shakuhachi* is a traditional Japanese flute which is played as you would a recorder. In the late 19th century, Japanese men were forbidden to carry weapons, so sometimes used their *shakuhachi* instead.

Cajun music, found in small communities in Louisiana, USA, is traditionally sung in French. The instruments used include the fiddle, an accordian, a guitar and either a triangle or spoons.

Qawwali music from India and Pakistan is the performance of sacred Sufi Muslim poetry. Performed at many religious festivals today, the foundation of the *qawwali* dates from the late 13th and early 14th century composer Amīr Khosrow.

Youssou N'Dour introduced the world to *mbalax*, a type of music from Senegal, in the 1990s. Sung in Wolof, the language of the Niger–Congo, *mbalax* mixes traditional Wolof music with Cuban and other Latin American musical styles.

Popular Mexican music includes traditional mariachi and ranchero songs, as well as modern hip hop and salsa.

Ladysmith Black Mambazo was founded in South Africa in 1964. Joseph Shabalala wanted to update traditional Zulu music. Performing at the time of apartheid, their music became globally known when Paul SImon featured them on his globally successful *Graceland* album and tour.

Drums are very important in Native American music. There are three types: single-headed drums, double-headed drums and kettle drums. Each drum is often decorated with tassels and pendants.

A popular form of music in Thailand is *phlaeng luk thung*, a version of Thai country music, sung in the fields by workers.

Cuban music combines both African and Spanish traditions, and is hugely popular with dancers. The rumba, cha-cha-cha and bolero are all key dance styles too.

The sound of music

Humans have been listening to music since we could bang two sticks together around a campfire, but in the 21st century there are many different ways to experience your favourite sounds.

Technology now means you have access to the whole world's music via your mobile phone. Or you can watch a concert in Korea live-streamed to your bedroom.

Alternatively you can listen to someone play live. Go to a gig in a community hall, or watch a huge band from a stadium seat.

Whatever you do, it will always be music to your ears.

What an atmosphere!

Fans of live music always talk about the atmosphere you experience when listening to a band or an orchestra play live. The performer connects with their audience and transmits how they are feeling right at that moment.

Street performers

Playing music on the streets, or busking, is one way to practise playing in public.

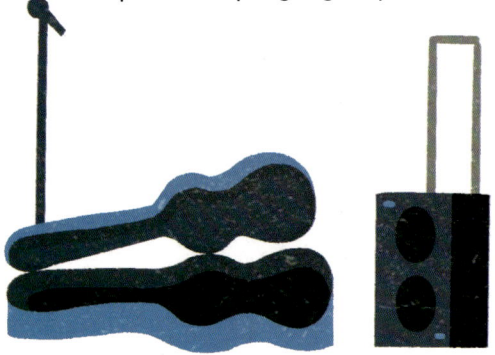

Music club

Starting out is easier in a small venue. Clubs and cafes often want musicians to entertain their customers.

Concert hall

Once you've created demand and have an audience willing to pay for tickets to hear you play, you might end up in a concert hall.

Stadium tour

The biggest bands and performers may well put on a stadium tour, where they play to thousands of people at a time.

Famous venues

There are music venues in most towns and cities across the globe. Here are some of the more well-known places to listen to live music.

Originally built by P.T. Barnum, Madison Square Garden, New York, USA, now hosts sports events and ice shows as well as musical concerts.

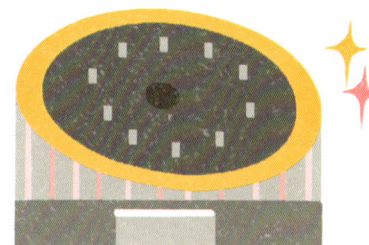

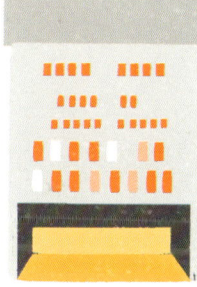

The Opera House in Sydney, Australia, is one of the most iconic venues in the world.

The Royal Albert Hall, London, UK, was built by Queen Victoria in memory of her husband Prince Albert.

Japan's Nippon Budokan Hall in Tokyo is an octagonal building which was originally used for martial arts.

L'Olympia, Paris, France, was built in 1888 as a music hall.

The Grosser Musikvereinssaal, Vienna, Austria, has 2,000 seats and six different music halls.

Red Rocks Amphitheatre, Colorado, USA, is a large, outdoor venue with stunning natural acoustics.

Dalhalla, Rättvik, Sweden, is another open-air venue situated in a limestone quarry.

Ronnie Scott's jazz club in London, UK, attracts jazz lovers from all over the world.

And try that one more time...

While recorded music may not have the immediate emotional connection that a live performance does, it is certainly much more accessible and easy to listen to on the device of your choosing.

Although it may be incredibly easy for anyone to record music on their laptop in their bedroom with today's technology, it hasn't always been that way. Early ways of recording music used mechanical objects such as a hand-wound cylinder that had pins which struck a keyboard or a piano roll that had perforated holes through which air was blown to strike the keys. However, this all changed with the invention of the phonograph, or record player.

A record player reproduces sounds that are created by the vibrations of a stylus, or needle, which follows the grooves embedded in a vinyl record. The sounds are 'recorded' in the surface of the vinyl disc and can then be replayed by another stylus.

Invented in 1877 by Thomas Edison in the form of a cylinder, it was Emil Berliner in 1887 who came up with the flat disc that some people still use today. By taking a negative of the recording, it was possible to produce copies of the record.

Over the next 75 years, improvements were made to both the record player and the recording process itself, but it wasn't until 1958 that stereo sound became a commercial reality.

Records were largely replaced by cassettes in the 1970s and 1980s, and then compact discs (CDs) in the 1990s. Now, most people use apps to stream music from their computer or their smart phone.

Recording music also allows the artist or performer to polish and correct any imperfections before releasing their music to consumers. Here sound engineers and mixers become very important.

Often they will have multiple tracks or layers to combine or 'mix' into one piece of music. In the recording studio, different elements will be recorded separately. The sound engineer can then add special sound effects such as reverb or fade to these different elements before creating the final 'mix'.

The benefits of recorded music

It is easy to listen to a huge range of musical genres.

Music is more accessible to more people.

You can listen to musicians who you would never be able to hear live.

The connection between music and listener can be stronger as there is nothing to interfere.

Careers in music

There are many different careers in the music industry! It takes more than just a musician to put a tour or album together. How many of these roles have you heard of?

Musical artist

Songwriter

DJ

Composer

Musical director

Radio producer

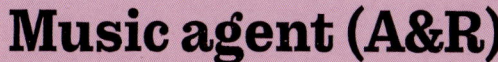
Music agent (A&R)

Concert promoter

Tour manager

Music producer

Sound engineer

Music tutor

Music journalist

Music therapist

Find out about all these different careers on the following pages! What would you like to do?

Musical artist

There are many different ways a musician can work in the music industry. From a solo pop star to a session musician, from a virtuoso classical soloist to a cover band musician, from a singer-songwriter to a member of an orchestra, all these roles require musical talent.

A classical soloist or rock star

These are musical artists at the top of their game. They have worked hard to reach this position and enjoy the rewards of their success. Audiences around the world flock to see them perform in concert halls and arenas.

A session musician, backing singer or ensemble member

These musicians and singers provide support to the solo artists, either on tour, in a recording studio or in single performances.

Orchestras, such as the New York Philharmonic or the London Symphony Orchestra, will have permanent members.

Session musicians can be hired for short-term projects such as recording an album or soundtrack.

Backing singers are extremely versatile and are able to pick up a part with little or no rehearsal.

A singer-songwriter

These performing songwriters write and record their own original music. With the advent of new technologies and streaming, more people than ever are writing their own music and making it available for everyone to listen to. These musicians want to share their musical identity by expressing their personality through their music.

What skills do you need to be a musical artist?

You should be talented musically.

You should be prepared to work hard.

You should be good at communication.

You should be ambitious.

You must be able to handle criticism.

You must love performing in public.

You should be good at motivating yourself.

Composer

Composers create music to be played by bands or orchestras. Covering types such as classical, jazz or opera, composers write music for performance, or to accompany a visual element, such as a film soundtrack.

Composers piece together different elements to deliver something new. They work with melody, rhythm, musical structure and energy to create a finished work.

Sometimes composers are asked to create a specific piece of music to go with action on screen, or to celebrate an event, such as a wedding or coronation.

What skills do you need to be a composer?

You need to be able to compose a tune.

You should be able to read and write music.

You should understand music theory.

You must be happy working on your own without the need for others.

Songwriter

The songwriter or lyricist is the person who puts words to music — for a song, an advertising jingle or a Broadway musical. Sometimes they are performers too, and create their own music. Songwriters often have to work with many different musical styles.

What skills do you need to be a songwriter?

You need to be able to write a good song.

You should be a storyteller.

You should understand current music trends and know how to play with them.

An understanding of melody and harmony is crucial.

It's helpful if you can play an instrument such as a keyboard or guitar.

45

DJ

DJs use their musical knowledge, the latest technology and software, plus an understanding of what their audience wants to hear to create fantastic dance sets that get the crowd jumping.

They also remix tracks by other artists to create a dance version of their songs.

Most DJs use software to mix their music. They speed up or slow down the intros and outros so the music is seamless. Some use different effects such as looping to change how a track sounds.

DJs work in clubs or at festivals. Some DJs are mobile and play at parties or weddings. Other DJs work for radio stations or record podcasts to engage music fans.

What skills do you need to be a DJ?

You need to have awareness of musical trends.

You should be good with music editing software and music production.

To perform as a live DJ, it is helpful to have great stage presence.

It's helpful if you enjoy networking with people too.

Radio producer

A radio producer or content director manages the content played on a radio station.

Working with DJs, the music director and programme makers, a radio producer ensures there is a consistent voice across the different shows. They help to shape the radio station's identity – what it is known for – and attract new listeners. They are in charge of the station's schedule as well as working with writers to develop new content.

What skills do you need to be a radio producer?

This is a role for someone with lots of experience who has already worked in radio for several years.

You should be good at critical thinking and working well under pressure.

You need to have leadership skills and the ability to manage people.

You should be able to budget, schedule and be used to hiring people.

Musical director

A musical director is responsible for shaping every part of a musical performance.

This could be a musical theatre production or a band on tour. They could work for a music festival or a particular venue.

Preparing for a show, the musical director will audition and hire the musicians needed. They will organise and direct rehearsals making sure everyone knows exactly what their role is.

Their musical knowledge is key to ensuring the correct feel of the performance.Sometimes they even end up playing during the performance. Some musical directors create the arrangements that the musicians play.

During a performance, the musical director cues the musicians. They are also responsible for managing any live technical or musical issues.

They have to communicate any changes in the set to the band or musicians and sometimes even manage their pay.

What skills do you need to be a musical director?

You need to have a broad knowledge of musical instruments.

You should be used to creating musical arrangments.

You must be good with people and a successful negotiator.

You must be organised and a good communicator.

You must work well in a team, but have good leadership skills.

Music agent

Music agents work with their clients — musical artists or performers — to schedule concerts, tours and in-person appearances. The agent is responsible for negotiating the fees and contracts for each of those bookings, and in return they earn a commission. They may also be called a talent agent or a booking agent.

For new clients who are just starting out, the agent will need to work hard to find slots as a supporting act, or a series of club events to build their artist's profile.

For bigger or famous artists, it might be easier for the agent to book a gig, but there could also be advertising deals or sponsorship to negotiate. National or global tours, as well as radio or TV appearances, are also a possibility.

It's important for a music agent to develop good relationships with promoters, festival organisers, venue managers and bookers in their client's chosen genre. They need to understand what each venue requires and how their client can support that venue.

Agents work very closely with their clients and it is their job to ensure that the artist is looked after while performing. That can sometimes include booking travel or hotel rooms and organising food.

What skills do you need to be a music agent?

You need to have strong written and verbal communication skills.

You must be a good negotiator and understand contracts.

You need to be confident and assertive.

You must be organised, be able to multitask and pay attention to detail.

Being a people person and good at managing relationships is also essential.

51

Music producer

A music, or record, producer works with an artist to record their music according to the artist's vision. It is their role to guide the artist to create the best version of their track or performance possible.

A music producer is often hired because they can demonstrate they have delivered previous projects on time and on budget. That might be a large-scale project – the new album from a best-selling artist – or a new indie artist who is inexperienced in the recording process and requires support.

Before entering the recording studio, a music producer will have worked on the score, hired session musicians and recording engineers, and scheduled out the sessions.

Music producers work with their artist or musicians to get the very best performance from them. They approve each element created and then select the right take, backing or solo performance.

It's important that the producer manages the right atmosphere in the recording studio. Performers need to believe in themselves and so a producer must project an air of confidence and positivity at all times.

They then take the initial vocal and instrumental recordings and, working with a sound or mixing engineer, they combine the tracks into a finished piece. It often takes longer to create the final mix than it does to record the music in the first place.

What skills do you need to be a music producer?

You should have a thorough knowledge of music.

You need to be an effective project manager.

You should have amazing listening skills.

You must be able to use recording technology, or at least understand what it can do.

You must be able to manage a schedule and a budget.

Concert promoter

In the live music industry, concert promoters are the people responsible for making many live events happen.

They work with artists and venues to create a live experience for the audience. Because they take on the financial risk of the project, they are very focused on numbers. They balance the costs associated with putting on a performance – the marketing, ticket sales, fees for the artist and the venue, the cost of the team who sets up the stage and takes it down again, the set, the travel and transportation costs as well as hotel bills – with the money they will receive from ticket sales. If they are any goood at their job, they will make a profit.

What skills do you need to be a concert promoter?

You need to understand budgets and be good with numbers.

You should have a great eye for detail, and be able to multitask.

You must understand contracts and be a good negotiator.

It's important to be a good communicator and very organised.

Zoom IN

Tour manager

Tour managers are employed by record companies or musicians to manage their live tours.

They are responsible for ensuring everything runs smoothly – from travel plans to media interviews, from food and accommodation while on tour to coordinating the load-in, sound check and set times.

A tour manager is also responsible for managing the budget assigned to the tour, and making any problem disappear.

What skills do you need to be a tour manager?

You need to be extremely well organised and efficient.

You should be great at networking, work well with people and able to defuse difficult situations.

You need to work well under pressure and be able to make quick decisions.

Sound engineer

The right levels of sound are very important to music production, whether it is live or recorded. Sound engineers work with mixing consoles to make sure that every element of the music is heard the way the artist wants it to be.

Live sound mix engineer

A live sound mix engineer will meet with the artist or band before the show. They need to understand key moments in the performance and any special requests the band may have.

The musicians will perform a sound check where the engineer sets the initial levels.

During the performance, the engineer needs to react quickly and make minor adjustments as the music plays to ensure that the performers and the audience hear what they are supposed to.

Mixing engineer

The major difference between a live sound engineer and a mixing engineer is that one has the luxury of being able to say 'Just one more time!'.

The mixing engineer works closely with the recording artist or musicians. Sitting in the sound booth at the mixing desk, they focus on individual notes to ensure that the singer hits the exact one. They record instruments and voices separately and then combine the different tracks together, mixing them to create just the right balance.

A mixing engineer can also add special effects such as 'delay' or 'reverb' to the music to enhance the final piece.

What skills do you need to work in sound?

You must be able to use a sound-editing programme and understand sound systems.

You should have a superb ear for music and be able to hear tiny details.

You should be good at networking and collaborating with your artists.

You need to be reliable and able to focus for long periods of time.

Music tutor

Music tutors, or teachers, help people learn how to play musical instruments or sing. They teach people of all ages and abilities. Some music tutors work with professional musicians to improve their skills, others teach children how to play their first musical instrument.

To be able to teach people how to play music, a music tutor needs to be able to play an instrument or sing well themselves. They will need to have qualifications that prove they are good enough.

A music tutor will often have to demonstrate how to play pieces of music to their students when they teach. Often a music tutor will be able to play more than one instrument.

Sometimes they will need to accompany their pupils during examinations or audtitions on the piano or the guitar.

As well as teaching the practical skills involved in playing an instrument or singing and reading music, music tutors also teach their pupils the theory of music. How music works, what a note is, what a scale or chord might be. They also teach music history, composition (how to write music) and about composers.

Music tutors in schools often lead the school band, orchestra or choir, and help support the drama department when putting on school productions.

Music tutors play a very important role in ensuring that music continues in our culture. They support aspiring musicians, but even if their pupils aren't going to become the next Taylor Swift, there are huge benefits in learning about and enjoying music for everyone, such as:

self-expression

fine motor skills

improved memory

improved language skills

improved confidence

making friends

shared experiences

What skills do you need to be a music tutor?

You must be able to play the musical instrument you wish to teach.

If you want to be a vocal coach, you must be a good singer.

You need to work well with others and encourage people to learn.

You must be able to organise your schedule and plan your lessons.

You may well be self-employed so you must be good at motivating yourself.

You should be able to use musical software and apps, and be aware of the latest technology.

Music therapist

Music therapists use music and how we respond to it to help people with physical, emotional, behavioural and social needs. Music can help to manage pain, improve memory, express emotion and reduce stress.

Music therapists work within the health and well-being sector and so need to be properly qualified to do so. Because they work with patients who may not be very well, it is important that they have had training and experience working in this area.

Each patient may require a different solution, so the music therapist will work with their patients to understand their goals, and then create a music programme to help them.

This could include creating or writing music, rehearsing and then performing, or simply listening to music and writing down how it makes them feel.

Most music therapists start with a degree in music therapy and then will need to take a professional qualification that allows them to practise as a therapist. Once qualified, they could work privately with individual patients or as part of a medicial or educational facility. They also must undertake ongoing professional development to ensure that they know of new developments and research.

Music therapy is a growing field as the positive impact of music on people's mental well-being can't be dismissed. Music therapists work with doctors, social workers, teachers, psychologists and psychiatrists to support their patients.

What skills do you need to be a music therapist?

You must be able to play the guitar, piano and percussion instruments, as well as sing.

You should be able to compose and arrange songs and music.

You need to be able to assess your patients and plan their treatment.

You may well need to conduct research to determine the best course of treatment for your patient.

You should have strong interpersonal skills and be emotionally intelligent.

Zoom IN

Music journalist

One of the best ways to experience music for free is to become a music journalist, or blogger, or reporter, or critic! You get to turn up to events or even hear new music before anyone else in order to tell the rest of the world what you think about it.

A music journalist might specialise in a particular kind of music. Some might cover local bands, others look out for brand-new artists or write in-depth articles on classic albums.

The one thing you all have in common is that you love to listen. Once you've listened, then it's time to write.

Most of your day is spent at your computer. You will be in contact with record company publicists whose job it is to keep you up to date with whatever is happening with their artists. You might be researching information on how a band was formed or what is popular in a certain age group. You could be writing up the gig you went to the night before.

Speaking of gigs, most music journalists are night owls, attending concerts or watching bands perform late into the night.

Your contacts are hugely important. To get a scoop on a brand-new release or some juicy gossip about a band member requires you to be on first-name terms with those publicists.

How to start

Unfortunately the best way to become a music journalist is to **be** a music journalist – only without being paid!

Start reviewing music or gigs and send them to your local online paper.

Or start a blog and grow your visibility that way.

What skills do you need to be a music journalist?

You need to be passionate about music and have a pretty good general knowledge about the subject.

You should be curious and interested in finding new stories to share with your readers.

You should have great writing skills and the ability to retain information.

You need to be quick on your feet and be able to think outside the box.

You should be a great self-motivator as many music journalists are self-employed and deadlines are important.

How to create music

If you have the talent and ability to play a musical instrument or write a song, there have never been more opportunities for you to do so.

21st century technology combined with your creativity means that you can enjoy playing, creating and performing music for everyone to hear and see.

Read on to find out how...

to write a song...

to record your music...

to form a band...

and to put on a musical performance.

How to write a song...

Now you've learned all about what it takes to be a musician, it's your turn. Follow these step-by-step instructions and you'll be creating music in no time.

1. Choose your subject

There are songs about sunshine, there are songs about elephants, there are songs for when you are sad and there are songs for when you are happy. Decide what you want to write your song about as that will give you a great place to start.

2. Choose your musical genre

Once you know what you want to write about, that helps to narrow down the musical genre you should use. If your subject is happy, then upbeat pop could work. If your subject is angry, then a rock theme might help. Will your subject suit a slow tempo or a fast beat?

3. Write a chorus melody

Use your favourite instrument or sing some notes that you can put together into a catchy chorus melody. Normally a chorus is four lines long, with repeating melodies. If you're stuck, listen to some of your favourite songs to see how they are put together.

4. Work out your song structure

Once you have the building blocks of the subject, genre and a great chorus, you need to decide the shape of your song. In most popular songs, there are usually two or three verses, broken up with the chorus. The chorus can repeat also. Will three verses be enough for you to get across everything you want to say?

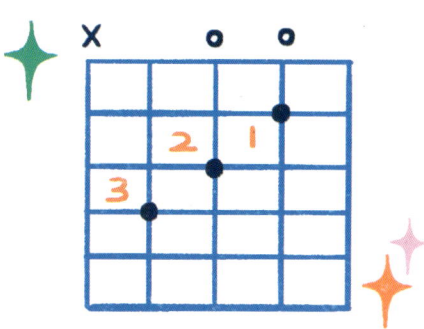

5. Write the chord structure or progression

Now you have your chorus melody and your structure, you can work out the chords to underpin the song. Are you in a major or minor key? Most pop songs use a four chord progression as a foundation. Choose which four you want to work with.

6. Write the verse melody

If you have a four line chorus, it's a good idea to have a four line verse. The verse melody should be different to the chorus melody. Here's a simple trick to help form the verse.

i. Create your first line melody.

ii. For the second line, repeat the shape of the melody but move it slightly higher in range.

iii. The third line should be different so it contrasts.

iv. The fourth line should repeat the first line.

7. Write the lyrics

Now you have the melodies, you need to put some words to the song. When writing the chorus, it's a good idea to include the title of the song either at the beginning or as the last thing you hear. Like when telling a story, It's also important for the song to have a beginning, a middle and an end.

8. Finish the connecting pieces

Would you like a bridge – a section of music that contrasts with the rest of the song? How will you start your song? How will you finish your song? Work out these answers and then put it all together.

9. Sing it out loud

If this is the first time you've written a song, well done! How do you feel about it? Once you've practised it a couple of times, ask a friend or family member to listen to it, or record it on your phone so you can hear it without having to concentrate on playing. What do you like? What could you change to improve it?

How to record your music

If you happen to be a successful pop star already, you would pop into your local recording studio to lay down your latest track, but most of us don't have access to one of those. Here is how to set up your own basic space at home and how to record your song so the world can hear it.

1. A quiet space

The first thing you will need is a quiet place to record. Soundproof would be brilliant, but that's unlikely at home. Your school might have a recording studio you could use, but if not, persuade your family to go out for a while and shut all the windows.

2. Your equipment

To take advantage of the latest technology, you will need a laptop or computer. You will also need a microphone, ideally with pop filters (to cut out the hard-sounding consonants when singing). If you are using electronic instruments, such as a guitar, you will need an amplifier. You can simply rely on a microphone plugged into your computer, but if you have access to an audio interface, it's worth borrowing one as it plugs into your laptop and all the audio feeds plug into it.

3. Download your digital audio workstation (DAW)

This is a really useful tool that allows you to record, edit and mix the different audio tracks that you will record. There are plenty available online and the trick is to choose one that is simple to use. If you use a Mac, Garageband is free to use and user-friendly. If you are on a PC, try Audacity which is also free and has plenty of online tutorials to help you get started.

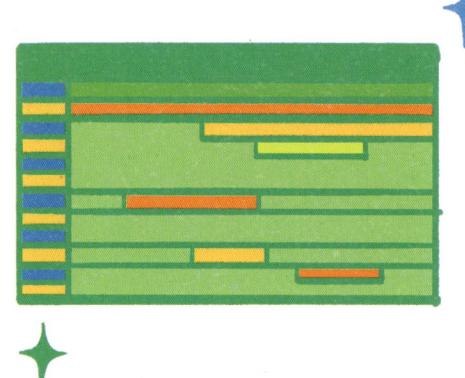

4. Plan your recording schedule

Most artists split out the different elements of their song to record them individually. This gives great control over the quality of the finished song. Each track is recorded at the same tempo or beat, and obviously in tune with each other. Normally the order would be as follows:

base track

rhythm

harmony

melody/vocals

background vocal

any special in-fills or effects

5. Set up and test your equipment

Check the connections between all your equipment and test for volume. Make a short recording of each element to make sure they sound the way you want them to.

6. Make your base track

This is not your bass guitar! This is the base beat track that will make you keep all your other tracks to tempo. You can download a simple metronome, or create one yourself. It simply needs to match the tempo you want.

7. Start recording

It's time to start recording your song. Follow the order above and take your time. Remember, the benefit of recorded music over live performance is that you can have as many tries as you need. When recording each track, listen to the base track through headphones to make sure you keep in time. Save each file as you go, and don't record over any of them. Use a simple file-naming convention so you know which file is which.

9. Mix your track

Once all your tracks are recorded, load them into your DAW and keep them organised. Listen to the track. Can you hear the rhythm section? Is the guitar or keyboard louder than the vocal? Does the backing vocal drown out the main one? Music producers will use terms such as equalising, compressing and panning which simply put means to balance out the levels in your song. Play around with the software to work out what sounds best. When you're happy, export your track!

How to form a band

If you love music, you might want to play in a band. This is different to a classical orchestra or school brass band. This is often a small group of people, say four or five, who enjoy making music together. It's really easy to form your own too!

1. Choose your genre

Before you can decide who will be in your band, you need to decide what sort of music you want to play. Will you be writing your own material or will you perform cover versions of other people's songs? While you can perform cover versions live for free, if you want to record that song and sell it, you will need to pay royalties to the original songwriter/artist.

2. Decide which musicians you need

Once you've decide what type of music you want to play, that should help you work out whether you need guitar players, a keyboard player, a drummer or a fiddle player. How many vocalists do you want? Should the musicians also be able to sing? A standard rock band formation, for example, has a lead guitar, a rhythm guitar, a bass guitar and drums.

3. Hold auditions

Advertise for musicians and hold auditions. You could do this at school, or in a local community centre. Make sure to check that anyone auditioning understands the kind of songs you want to perform.

4. Rehearsal space

Once you have your band, you'll need to find somewhere to rehearse. You might be lucky enough to have space at home and an understanding family. Or perhaps you could borrow a garage from a neighbour? Wherever you end up, always be considerate about the noise you're making. Drums and guitars can be quite loud!

5. What equipment do you need?

If you want to perform live, you'll need to make sure you have the right equipment. Microphones for the vocals, plus any acoustic instruments being played. You'll also need amps for the microphones and any electric instruments. Most venues will have lighting, but sometimes it's helpful to have a few lights just to add focus!

6. Name your band!

You have a band, but what is it called? The name should be memorable and reflect the type of music you want to play. It can be hard to get everyone to agree so choose a shortlist of two and have everyone vote!

7. Create your set list

OK, so now you can choose the songs you want to learn and play. Why don't you create a short set list? Pick five or six songs that show off your skills. Order them so you start and finish with a bang!

8. Work out a rehearsal schedule

Now it's time to practise, practise, practise! Each member of the band needs to practise at home too so that they know their parts perfectly. Then, when rehearsing, you can focus on making the whole sound good. Don't forget to have fun! If you didn't know your fellow band mates well before, you will after eight weeks of rehearsals!

9. Set yourselves a goal

The best bit about being in a band is performing in front of an audience. Pick a date, arrange a performance, or perhaps there's a school event you could play at? Give yourselves something to aim for and then go out on stage and enjoy!

How to put on a music gig

Once you have your band, it's time to stage your first performance. There's nothing more exciting than striding out on stage and wowing your audience with your music!

1. Choose your venue

Once you've decided to show off your band's new-found skills, you need to find somewhere to do so. You could maybe use your school hall or gym, or perhaps hire a local community centre. Check the venue of your choice has a licence for live music performance.

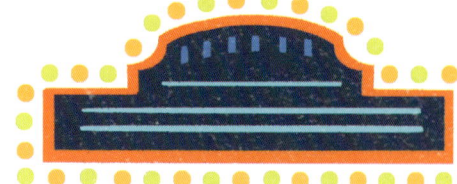

2. Select your dates

You might be well-rehearsed and able to perform immediately but it's good to have four weeks or so to be able to advertise your gig to the community. Make sure it doesn't clash with anything big like a key sports fixture or other social event in the area.

3. Refine your set list

Work out which songs you want to sing and in what order to make the most impact. You might want to consider involving other local bands too to increase the size of the potential audience.

4. Sell those tickets

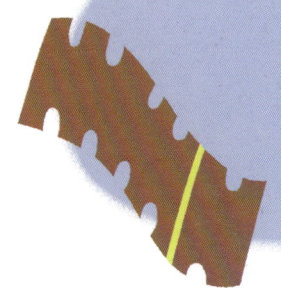

There is no point putting on a gig if there is no audience. You need to make people aware that your gig is happening. Ask friends and family to put up posters around the community. Encourage them to sell tickets for a reasonable price. You may need to recover the cost of hiring the venue. Once you've covered your costs, you could donate the rest of the profits to a charity of your choice.

5. Final rehearsal

This is the last rehearsal before your gig. You'll need someone to help you adjust the sound levels on the night, so they should definitely attend this rehearsal. Use this time to make sure the band know how to act between songs, and work out how you are going to introduce the band to the audience.

6. Sound check

It's the day of the gig! You'll need to set up your equipment and make sure all the connections are working. This is called a sound check. Make sure you have a few friends along to help carry equipment and give you moral support.

7. It's showtime!

Here you go! All your hard work, and that of your band and crew, has been building up to this moment. You should always announce your entrance. Keep it simple, 'Ladies and gentlemen, we are [insent band name here]!' You can also introduce each song, especially if it's your own work.

7. Encore, encore

You've had a successful gig. The audience are on their feet whooping and clapping in appreciation. It's time for the encore. Most bands leave the stage and then come back for one last crowdpleaser. Make sure you have one ready in case you need it.

8. The get out

After the final song, there's still work to be done. You need to remove all your equipment from the venue. The ticket sales need adding up and the proceeds shared with the right people. You should be proud of yourself and your band! And even better, the venue has just rebooked you! Congratulations!

How to get started...

There are lots of ways to get involved in music:

Learn an instrument or take singing lessons.

Join a school choir, band or orchestra.

Make music in your bedroom and share it with the world.

Form your own band.

Learn how to DJ.

If you're more interested in the technical aspects of music production, then approach your local music venues to find out what work experience they offer.

You can do so much online too. There are some fabulous resources (see page 76 and 77) that will give you even more information than this book does.

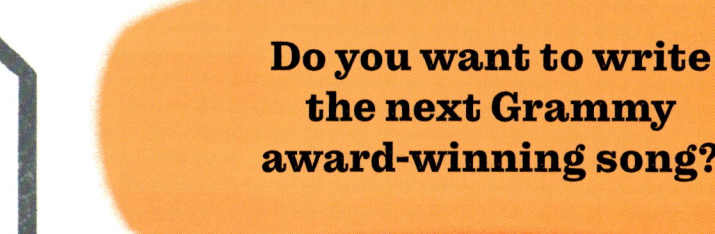

Do you want to write the next Grammy award-winning song?

Would you like to become a music journalist and review gigs?

Would you like to represent the best musical artists in the world?

Why not compose the soundtrack to the next few years of your life?

Would you like to help people by using music?

Be inspired, be creative, be organised.

But most of all, get involved and keep trying.

Further reading

There are plenty of really fabulous websites with lots more resources than we could fit into this book. Check out the following:

www.musicweek.com

www.musicindustryhowto.com

www.careersinmusic.com

www.berklee.edu/careers

www.ram.ac.uk

Acknowledgements

With thanks to the following people:

Music teacher extraordinaire, Rachel Bee, for being kind enough to read through this and check for errors. Any remaining are entirely down to the writer!

Harrogate Secondary Schools Orchestra and North Yorkshire County Youth Orchestra for supporting my musical endeavours during my teenage years.

Pauline Dunn, my cello teacher, who terrified me into practising, and Mr Mills, my piano teacher, who encouraged me with a smile.

Index

Page numbers such as 54-56 show page ranges, where you will find information about the topic on all the pages between page 54 and page 56.

accordions 32
African American music 27, 28
African music and instruments 17, 30, 32, 33
American traditional music and instruments 17, 33
anthems (pop songs) 24
auditions 48, 58, 70

backing singer (job role and skills) 42, 43
bands (how-to guide) 70–71
bass tracks 69
bassoons 11, 14
Beatles, the 22
blues 27
boogie-woogie 29
booking agent (job role and skills) 50–51
brass instruments 10–11, 15
Britpop 23
busking 7, 36

Cajun traditional music and instruments 32
careers (job roles and skills) 40–63
Caribbean music 29
castanets 16, 31
cellos 11, 13
changgo (drum) 30
Chinese traditional music and instruments 12, 30
choirs 7, 59, 74
clappers (percussion instruments) 16
clarinets 10, 14
classical composers 18–19

classical music (development of) 8
classical musician (job role and skills) 42, 43
composer (job role and skills) 44
composers (timeline) 18–19
concert halls 36, 37
concert promoter (job role and skills) 54
conductor 10–11
cor anglaises 11
country music 20, 26
Cuban music 33
cymbals 16

Dalhalla open-air venue (Rättvik) 37
dance 25, 28, 31, 33
digital audio workstation (DAW) 68, 69
disco 20, 25
DJ (job role and skills) 46
DJs (hip hop) 28
double basses 11, 13, 27
drums 10–11, 17, 30, 31, 33

electric guitars and other instruments 23, 68, 71
encores 73

festivals 23, 32, 46, 48, 51
film soundtracks 44
flutes (orchestral) 10, 14
flutes (traditional Japanese) 31
folk music 20, 26
funk 20, 28

glockenspiels 16
gospel music 27
Grosser Musikvereinssaal music halls (Vienna) 37
grunge 23
guitars 7, 22, 23, 26, 29, 32

harmony 6
harps 10, 12, 30

heavy metal 23
Hendrix, Jimi 23
hip hop 20, 28, 32
horns 10, 15

improvised music 27
Indian traditional music and instruments 31, 32
Islamic music 31, 32

Japanese traditional music and instruments 31
jazz 13, 14, 20, 27, 37
jingxi (Peking opera) 30

K-Pop (Korean pop) 25
kettle drums (timpani) 11, 17, 33
Korean traditional music and instruments 30

Ladysmith Black Mambazo 33
Latin American music 32
listening to music 34–39
live music 36–37, 42, 48–49, 54–56, 62–63
live music (how-to guide) 72–73
lutes 12, 30
lyres 12, 30

Madison Square Garden (New York) 37
marching/military bands 15, 16
Marley, Bob 29
mbalax music (Senegal) 32
medieval period 8, 18
melody 6
Mexican music 32
microphones 68, 71
military/marching bands 15, 16
mixing music 28, 39, 46, 53, 56–57, 69
Motown 20, 27
music agent (job role and skills) 50–51

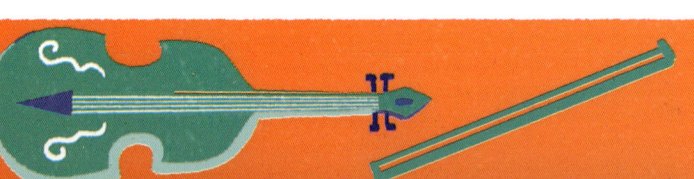

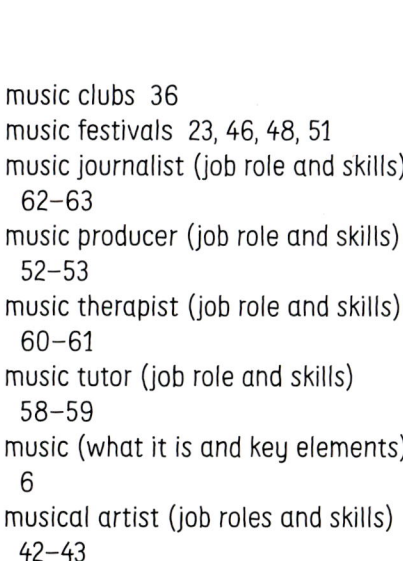

music clubs 36
music festivals 23, 46, 48, 51
music journalist (job role and skills) 62–63
music producer (job role and skills) 52–53
music therapist (job role and skills) 60–61
music tutor (job role and skills) 58–59
music (what it is and key elements) 6
musical artist (job roles and skills) 42–43
musical director (job role and skills) 48–49

Nippon Budokan Hall (Tokyo) 37

oboes 11, 14
L'Olympia music hall (Paris) 37
opera 40, 44
orchestral musician (job role and skills) 42, 43
orchestras 7, 10–11

Pakistani traditional music 32
Peking opera 30
percussion instruments 10–11, 16–17, 30, 31, 33
phlaeng luk thung (Thai music) 33
pianos 11, 12, 27
piccolos 10, 14
political/protest music 26, 27, 29
Polynesian traditional music 31
pop music 20, 24–25
pop stars 24, 25
pot drums 17
Presley, Elvis 22
progressive rock 23
punk 23

qawwali music (India and Pakistan) 32

radio producer (job role and skills) 47
radio work 46, 47
ragtime 20, 27
rap music 20, 28
rattles 17
recorded music 38–39, 52–53, 57
recording your own music (how-to guide) 68–69
records and record players 38–39
Red Rocks Amphitheatre (Colorado) 37
reed instruments 14
reggae music 20, 29
rehearsals 48, 70, 71, 73
rhythm 6, 24, 28–29
rhythm section 13, 16
rock 22–23
rock star (job role and skills) 42, 43
rock 'n' roll 20, 22
Rolling Stones 23
Ronnie Scott's jazz club (London) 37
Royal Albert Hall (London) 37
royalties 70

sackbuts (early trombones) 15
salsa 32
saxophones 14, 27
session musician (job role and skills) 42, 43
set lists 71, 72
shakuhachi (flute) 31
singer-songwriter (job role and skills) 43, 45
sitar (stringed instrument) 31
ska 29
snare drums 17
solo musician (job role and skills) 42, 43
songwriter (job roles and skills) 43, 45
songwriting (how-to guide) 66–67
soul music 20, 27
sound check 55, 56, 73

sound engineer (job role and skills) 56–57
Spanish traditional music and instruments 31
special effects 39, 46, 57, 69
spoons 32
stadiums 36
streaming services 20, 39
street performers 7, 36
string quartets 8–9
stringed instruments 10–11, 12–13, 30, 31
Sydney Opera House 37

tabla (drum) 31
talent agent (job role and skills) 50–51
tambourines 31
Thai music 33
ticket sales 54, 72, 73
timpani (kettle drums) 11, 17, 33
tour manager (job role and skills) 55
traditional music from around the world 30–33
triangles 17, 32
trombones 11, 15, 27
troubadours 8, 20
trumpets 10–11, 15, 27
tubas 11, 15
tubular chimes/bells 17

violas 10–11, 13
violins 10, 13, 26, 32

woodwind instruments 10–11, 14
work experience 74
world music (traditional) 30–33
writing about music 62–63

xylophones 10, 16

zithers 12, 30

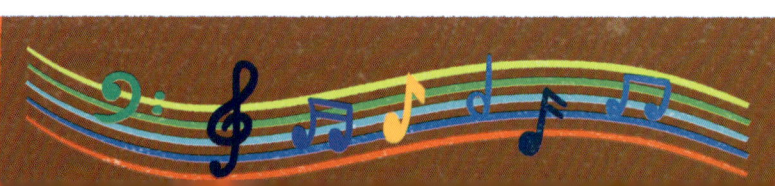

music clubs 36
music festivals 23, 46, 48, 51
music journalist (job role and skills) 62–63
music producer (job role and skills) 52–53
music therapist (job role and skills) 60–61
music tutor (job role and skills) 58–59
music (what it is and key elements) 6
musical artist (job roles and skills) 42–43
musical director (job role and skills) 48–49

Nippon Budokan Hall (Tokyo) 37

oboes 11, 14
L'Olympia music hall (Paris) 37
opera 40, 44
orchestral musician (job role and skills) 42, 43
orchestras 7, 10–11

Pakistani traditional music 32
Peking opera 30
percussion instruments 10–11, 16–17, 30, 31, 33
phlaeng luk thung (Thai music) 33
pianos 11, 12, 27
piccolos 10, 14
political/protest music 26, 27, 29
Polynesian traditional music 31
pop music 20, 24–25
pop stars 24, 25
pot drums 17
Presley, Elvis 22
progressive rock 23
punk 23

qawwali music (India and Pakistan) 32

radio producer (job role and skills) 47
radio work 46, 47
ragtime 20, 27
rap music 20, 28
rattles 17
recorded music 38–39, 52–53, 57
recording your own music (how-to guide) 68–69
records and record players 38–39
Red Rocks Amphitheatre (Colorado) 37
reed instruments 14
reggae music 20, 29
rehearsals 48, 70, 71, 73
rhythm 6, 24, 28–29
rhythm section 13, 16
rock 22–23
rock star (job role and skills) 42, 43
rock 'n' roll 20, 22
Rolling Stones 23
Ronnie Scott's jazz club (London) 37
Royal Albert Hall (London) 37
royalties 70

sackbuts (early trombones) 15
salsa 32
saxophones 14, 27
session musician (job role and skills) 42, 43
set lists 71, 72
shakuhachi (flute) 31
singer-songwriter (job role and skills) 43, 45
sitar (stringed instrument) 31
ska 29
snare drums 17
solo musician (job role and skills) 42, 43
songwriter (job roles and skills) 43, 45
songwriting (how-to guide) 66–67
soul music 20, 27
sound check 55, 56, 73

sound engineer (job role and skills) 56–57
Spanish traditional music and instruments 31
special effects 39, 46, 57, 69
spoons 32
stadiums 36
streaming services 20, 39
street performers 7, 36
string quartets 8–9
stringed instruments 10–11, 12–13, 30, 31
Sydney Opera House 37

tabla (drum) 31
talent agent (job role and skills) 50–51
tambourines 31
Thai music 33
ticket sales 54, 72, 73
timpani (kettle drums) 11, 17, 33
tour manager (job role and skills) 55
traditional music from around the world 30–33
triangles 17, 32
trombones 11, 15, 27
troubadours 8, 20
trumpets 10–11, 15, 27
tubas 11, 15
tubular chimes/bells 17

violas 10–11, 13
violins 10, 13, 26, 32

woodwind instruments 10–11, 14
work experience 74
world music (traditional) 30–33
writing about music 62–63

xylophones 10, 16

zithers 12, 30